Backyard Scientist®

Series Three

by Jane Hoffman

Illustrated by Lanny Ostroff

D0128471

Other works by Jane Hoffman:
"The Original Backyard Scientist." This widely read and popular book was the author's first writing effort and features many of the author's most popular experiments for children ages 4 through 12 years. **"Backyard Scientist, Series One."** The author's second book of science experiments provides children ages 4 through 12 with more fascinating and fun ways to explore the world of science. This book is a sequel to the first book and the beginning of a series of science books. **"Backyard Scientist, Series Two"**, is the author's third book of science experiments for ages 9 through 14 years and features a special collection of exciting, fascinating and challenging experiments.

Backyard Scientist, Series Three
Spring 1990
Library of Congress catalog card number: 90-080909
Published by Backyard Scientist/Jane Hoffman
Post Office Box 16966
Irvine, CA 92713
©1990 by Backyard Scientist/Jane Hoffman
All rights reserved. No portion of this book may be used or reproduced in any form or by any means without the express written permission of the publisher. Printed in the United States of America.

0-9618663-3-0

TABLE OF CONTENTS

Experiment	Page#

Introduction ————————————————————————————1

The Blinking Experiment - Concept Learned - Reflex actions versus learned actions ____2-3

The Digestion Experiment - Concept Learned - How enzymes help the body use food __4-5

The Vocal Cord Experiment - Concept Learned - Understanding your vocal cords _____6-7

The Muscle Experiment - Concept Learned - Muscles, how they work and
allow you to work ————————————————————————8-9

The Bird Experiment - Concept Learned -Making birdfeeders and classifying birds _____10-11

The Yeast Experiment - Concept Learned - Properties of yeast _____12-13

The Isopod Experiment - Concept Learned - Understanding the insect world _____14-15

The Backbone Experiment - Concept Learned - How our back allows us
to stand and bend ————————————————————————16-17

The Nerve Cell Experiment - Concept Learned - Understanding how
nerve cells operate ————————————————————————18-19

The Lung Experiment - Concept Learned - Understanding how our lungs operate _____20-21

The Ant Experiment - Concept Learned - The anatomy of an Ant _____22-23

The Ant Farm Experiment - Concept Learned - The Ant society _____24-25

Breathing Experiment - Concept Learned - Measuring your lung capacity_____26-27

Investigating Common Reflexes - Concept Learned - Understanding reflex actions _____28-29

Taste Buds Experiment - Concept Learned - Taste - Understanding a sense_____30 31

Earthworms Experiment - Concept Learned - Studying the simple Earthworm_____32-33

The Soil Experiment - Concept Learned - What is in your soil_____34-35

The Soil Test - Concept Learned - Understanding soil porosity _____36-37

The Ear Experiment - Concept Learned - Fun with sound_____38-39

The Leaf Experiment - Concept Learned - The importance of leaves to plant growth _____40-41

The Popcorn Experiment - Concept Learned - The parts of a popcorn kernel_____42-43

The Pulse Experiment - Concept Learned - What makes you tick _____44-45

The Vegetable and Fruit Experiment - Concept Learned - The effects of dehydration ____46-47

The Root Experiment - Concept Learned - The effects of gravity and light on seeds_____48-49

The Calcium Experiment - Concept Learned - Calcium and bone rigidity_____50-51

Backyard Scientist certificate information._____52

THE REVIEWS ARE IN ON BACKYARD SCIENTIST.

WHAT EDUCATORS AND PARENTS ARE SAYING ABOUT THE BACKYARD SCIENTIST

*"I just want to let you know how much we enjoy your book, **The Backyard Scientist.** As a mother of eight I really appreciate the clear instructions that allows a child to work independently from collecting materials through the questions that foster creative thinking and deductive reasoning. I'm waiting to see your next book."*
Jan Vreeland
Waukesha, Wisconsin

"I believe that you have many of the answers to our problems with science education in the early grades."
— Mary Kohleman,
National Science Foundation
Washington D.C.

"For the easiest and most enjoyable approach to science experiments, I recommend the Backyard Scientist and the new Backyard Scientist Series One, By Jane Hoffman."
— Mary Pride
The Teaching Home, June/July '87

"All the experiments are ones that are simple enough for a child to carry out himself (with a helpful parent nearby), and Jane is careful to use only materials commonly found around most homes. Often follow up ideas are given for further exploration and an explanation of the hows and whys."
— Susan Richman.
Pennsylvania Homeschoolers, June'87

"She makes science come alive."
Orange Coast Daily Pilot

"Backyard Scientist teaches children the art of thinking."
Anaheim Bulletin

Books offer a hands-on approach to elementary science.

*Two books from **Backyard Scientist (Irvine, CA)** originally designed for home schooling are proving to be effective classroom tools for a hands-on approach to teaching science at the elementary level. **The Original Backyard Scientist** and **Backyard Scientist, Series One** suggest experiments that are simple to perform yet demonstrate rather complex chemical and physical theories.*
As they make the worlds of chemistry and physics come alive, the experiments require students to use critical thinking skills. No exotic materials are necessary-only things commonly found in most homes.
Experiments contained in the two books are completely different.
Curriculum Product News
January, 1988

The Original Backyard Scientist
by Jane Hoffman

*This book (as well as Jane's second book **Backyard Scientist, Series One**) meets the needs of mothers who are looking for a science course with simple experiments and clear explanations. All of the experiments can be done, as the book says, "using things found around the house." What's more **Backyard Scientist** makes science fun for both teacher and child.*
*Even if you are working through a Science textbook, **The Backyard Scientist** can be an excellent supplemental book, aiding in the explanation of concepts dealing with Chemistry and Physics.*
***The Backyard Scientist** is Exceptional in its flexibility to be used with children, ages 4 through 12. This quality is especially helpful for those teaching multi-grade levels and/or using teaching methods. I would recommend this book to any family that wants science to be active, educational and fun.*
Reviewed by Roxanne Smith,
Grand Rapids, MI

Welcome to the world of the Life Sciences. Learn how your lungs operate, about reflex actions and the industrious ant to name just a few of the exciting experiments in this volume.

Thank you to my many supporters without who's encouragement this volume would not be a reality. I have enjoyed meeting the many young scientists and parents during my travels throughout the United States. To the many I have not yet had the pleasure to meet, I am sure we will as my travel plans expand each year.

Parents and teachers, I hope you will continue to encourage your youngsters to explore the world around them using this and the other Backyard Scientist books of hands-on experiments.

As soon as you begin experimenting, you become a Backyard Scientist working in the real world of scientific investigation. Your laboratory is wherever you are experimenting, be it in your backyard, kitchen or basement.

As a Backyard Scientist working in your laboratories, there are some very important guidelines you must follow.

1. Always work with an adult.
2. Never taste anything you are experimenting with except when instructed to do so in the experiment.
3. Always follow the Backyard Scientist directions In the experiment.
4. Always wash your hands with soap and warm water after you finish experimenting.
5. Be a patient scientist. Some experiments take longer than others before results can be observed.
6. If you have any questions about any of the experiments, write to me, Jane Hoffman, The Backyard Scientist, P.O. Box 16966, Irvine, CA 92713

You are ready to start experimenting. Have fun! When you complete all of the experiments be sure to read how to get your Backyard Scientist Certificate and how to join the Backyard Scientist Club. Details are at the back of the book.

Happy Experimenting,

Jane Hoffman

Your Friend,
Jane Hoffman
The Backyard Scientist

The Subject Matter of this work is based on the scientific. The author is specific in directions, explanations and warnings. If what is written is disregarded, failure or complication may occur - just as in the case in the laboratory. In the instances where flammable or toxic chemicals are involved, explicit explanation and warnings are provided.

1

THE BLINKING EXPERIMENT

Can you name one act that you did not have to learn to do?

Try the following Backyard Scientist experiment to discover the answer.

Gather the following supplies:

A friend to do the experiment with you, a square piece of plastic wrap, a piece of paper or cardboard, and six sheets of 8 1/2" by 11" paper.

Start Experimenting.

1. Take the paper or cardboard and make a frame for the plastic wrap so it is easier to handle.
2. Have your partner sit in a chair.
3. Take the six sheets of paper and crumple them into paper balls.
4. Have your partner hold the small piece of plastic wrap in front of his (or her) eyes and look straight at you.
5. Take the paper balls and gently throw each one against the sheet of plastic wrap. Did your partner blink?
6. Gather up the balls and repeat step 4. This time ask your partner to try to keep from blinking. You can repeat this as many times as you like.
7. Trade places, and have your partner throw paper balls at you, repeating the steps above.

Can you answer the following questions from your observation?

1. Did you blink each time the paper ball was thrown against the piece of plastic wrap?
2. Were you able to control your blinking?
3. Do you think you learned to blink when you were a baby?
4. Do you think blinking was an unlearned act?
5. Do you think you were able to blink the moment you were born?

Backyard Scientist solution to experiment.

You discovered that you blinked each time the ball was thrown against the piece of plastic wrap. You cannot control your blinking, because blinking is known as a reflex action. Reflex actions take place without a person having to think. These acts are part of your behavior from the time you are born. Blinking is an act you perform without having to learn. Blinking is an inborn, or unlearned act. Sneezing, coughing and yawning are three other inborn acts.

Additional investigations to do.

What other acts can you think of that can be performed without learning? If there is a new baby in your home, or at a friend's house, observe the baby's behavior. Make a list of all the unlearned acts the baby can perform. How do you know the baby's acts are un-learned? When do you think learning be-gins? Record the first, second , third and etc. acts that you think the baby has learned to perform. Did you know that today you may have blinked your eyelids more than 5,000 times?

Now explore the unlearned acts and learned acts with dogs, fish, and other pets that belong to you or your friends.

3

THE DIGESTION EXPERIMENT

Do you know how the food you eat is digested?

Try the following Backyard Scientist experiment to discover the answer.

Gather the following supplies:

Several unsalted soda crackers, 1 bottle of household iodine (remember iodine is a poison, an adult must help you with this), 1 plastic glass, (any size, half filled with water), 2 paper plates, 1 eyedropper (a straw can also be used as an eyedropper), and an adult to help you.

Start Experimenting.

1. Take one of the crackers and take a bite out of it.
2. How does it taste?
3. Continue to chew the cracker for two minutes. Don't swallow it. Now how does it taste?

Did you observe that at first the cracker tasted starchy, and after you chewed it for a couple of minutes it tasted sweet? Why do you think this happened?

4. Using the eyedropper or straw, have the adult take a few drops of iodine from the bottle and put it into the plastic glass with the water in it. You now have a diluted solution of iodine.
5. Take one of the crackers and wet it thoroughly with some plain water from the tap.
6. Put the cracker on a paper plate, and add a few drops of the iodine solution to the cracker. What happens?
7. Now take another cracker and chew it thoroughly without swallowing it until it begins to taste sweet.
8. Remove the chewed cracker from your mouth and put it on a paper plate.
9. Now add a few drops of the iodine solution to the cracker. What happens?

Can you answer the following questions from your observations?

1. Do you know why the cracker tastes starchy at first?
2. Do you know why, after you chewed the cracker for a few minutes, it tasted sweet? What made this happen?
3. When you put iodine on the wet cracker, do you know why it turned purple?
4. After you chewed the cracker and put the iodine on it why didn't it turn purple?

What does this tell you?
5. Do you know where digestion starts?
6. Do you know what the alimentary canal is?
7. Do you think animals have digestive systems?

Backyard Scientist solution to experiment.

The reason the wet cracker turned purple is because the cracker contains starch and putting the iodine on the cracker was a test for the presence of starch. Iodine turns purple in the presence of this chemical. An enzyme in your saliva helped change some of the starch in the cracker to sugar. This is why, after you chewed it, put it on the plate and tested it with iodine, it did not turn purple. There was no longer any starch in the cracker.

Enzymes help speed up digestion. Without them, the process would take much longer. Carbohydrates are broken down into sugars. Proteins are broken down into amino acids, and fats are broken down into glycerol and fatty acids. Saliva contains an enzyme which helps in the digestion of starch.

Once you have swallowed your food, it begins a long journey which ends in the cells. Digestion starts in the mouth and continues in the gut, or alimentary canal. All animals have some kind of a digestive system.

Now it might be fun to try the iodine test on other foods to see it they contain starch. Remember, always work with an adult when using iodine. Be sure to keep iodine away from all small children, and never eat the food that has the iodine on it, because iodine is a poison that can hurt you if swallowed.

5

THE VOCAL CORD EXPERIMENT

Can you compare a balloon to your vocal cords?

Try the following Backyard Scientist experiment to discover the answer.

Gather the following supplies:

1 balloon (any size).

Start Experimenting.

1. Blow up the balloon.
2. Pinch the mouth of the balloon to close it.
3. Spread the mouth and let the air out slowly.
4. Do you hear a sound?
5. Now try it again listening to the sound very carefully.
6. Blow up the balloon a few more times, and each time try to change the sound you hear. What do you have to do to the balloon to make a different sound?
7. Place your hand on your throat and hum. Do you feel vibrations? What do you think is vibrating?

Can you answer the following questions from your observations?

1. Were you able to change the pitch of the sound the balloon made? How?
2. Can you compare the balloon experiment you just did to your vocal cords?
3. What do you think caused the balloon to vibrate in the above experiment?
4. When you placed your hand on your throat and hummed, what do you think was vibrating?
5. Do your vocal cords vibrate when you are just breathing?
6. Make a high-pitched sound as high as you can go. Do your vocal cords feel close together or far apart?
7. Make a low humming noise. Do your vocal cords feel close together or far apart?
8. Do you know where your vocal cords are located?
9. When you hiccup, do you know what causes the strange noise you hear?
10. What other things affect the sound of your voice?
11. When you go to the dentist and he/she has to use anesthetic to freeze your mouth, can you speak well afterwards?

Backyard Scientist solution to experiment.

When you let the air out of the balloon you heard a sound. The pitch of the sound you heard can be varied by changing the tautness of the opening of the balloon. The above experiment demonstrates how moving air can cause something to vibrate and make sound. The end of the balloon can be compared to our vocal cords, with the moving air leaving the lungs. The sound you heard is being made by the vibrating open end of the balloon.

When you placed your hand on your throat and hummed, you could feel your throat vibrating. This is because the air from the lungs passes between the vocal cords. They vibrate, causing the air to vibrate. We detect the vibrating air as sound.

The vocal cords are two flaps of elastic tissue in the voice box or larynx. The larynx is an enlarged area at the upper end of the windpipe. The larynx is usually called the "adam's apple".

When your vocal cords are close together, high-pitched sounds are made. When vocal cords are open wide, low-pitched sounds are made. The vocal cords are relaxed during breathing and are not vibrating.

Hiccups are caused by your diaphragm contracting more violently than usual so that your in-breaths come in short gasps. The strange noise you hear is caused by your vocal cords suddenly closing. Nobody knows for sure why hiccups start.

Your throat, mouth, nose and nasal sinuses all add resonance to your voice. Children's sinuses are not completely developed, so their voices have a thinner, less rich quality than do the voices of adults. Your tongue and lips make the precise sounds of different words by altering the shape of your mouth. When your mouth has been anesthetized for dental work, you may find it hard to speak until the anesthetic wears off, and you get back control of your mouth muscles.

THE MUSCLE EXPERIMENT

Do you know why your muscles get tired?

Try the following Backyard Scientist experiment to discover the answer.

Gather the following supplies:

A book, a clothespin, a clock or watch with a second hand, and a chart on which to record your findings with the following headings: name, finger, hand, and arm, and a lot of friends to experiment with.

Start Experimenting.

1. Decide who will go first with the muscle test. Get the chart ready to record your findings.
2. Have someone ready to time the experiments.
3. First we are going to test our finger. Pick up the clothespin and hold the ends between your thumb and index finger.

Now find out how many times you can open and close the clothespin in 30 seconds. Be sure to open the clothespin completely each time you squeeze the ends together. Do this experiment three times and record your data on the chart. Have all the other people do this, one by one.

4. Now we are going to test our hand. Start again with the same person who went first last time. Put your arm on the table with the palm of your hand facing up. Find out how many times you can make a fist in 30 seconds. Be sure to open your hand completely, and then form a tight fist each time. Record your data on the chart. Have all the other people do this, one by one.

5. Now we are going to test our arm. Start again with the same person who went first last time. Pick up a book and stand with your hand holding the book hanging straight down. Find out how many times in 30 seconds you can lift the book to shoulder height. Keep your arm straight as you lift the book. Record your data on the chart. Have all the other people do this, one by one.

6. Do your muscles know when they are tired? How do they tell you?

Can you answer the following questions from your observations?

1. Did you get better or worse each time you repeated the experiments?
2. What could you do to improve the strength of the muscles you tested?
3. Do you think your muscles are different shapes and sizes?
4. Do you think your muscles work by themselves?
5. What other things do you think your muscles help you do?
6. Take a guess as to how many muscles you think are in your body.

Backyard Scientist solution to experiment.

When your muscles get tired or fatigued, it can mean many things. If your muscles get fatigued too quickly, it may mean that they are not getting enough exercise. Also, not eating the right diet will make you feel more fatigued.

Your muscles are different shapes and sizes, and they work in pairs. One muscle is pulling your bones back. When one muscle is working (contracting), the other muscle is relaxing. You have over 600 muscles in your body, and the muscles make up half the weight of your body.

The muscles are very important because they help hold your organs and skeleton in place and do their work. Your diaphragm muscle helps your lungs breathe, and your heart muscles make the blood flow through your body.

Your muscles help you chew food and close your eyelids. Muscles help you run and play and even smile and frown.

It is very important to take good care of your muscles and rest and relax periodically, because your muscles get tired too. If you sit too long in an uncomfortable position, you will feel cramped and certain places will ache. This is one way your muscles are telling you they have been working too long in one position, and they want to relax.

Muscles are fascinating. You may want to learn more by going to the library and doing some research on muscles.

You may want to test your muscles further by tying a weight around your foot to see how many times you can lift it. Try tying different weights and see how your muscles react.

THE BIRD EXPERIMENT

What do you know about birds?

Try the following Backyard Scientist experiment to discover the answer.

Gather the following supplies:

Two-2 quart size milk or orange juice cartons, something that will cut the carton, strong string or rope that is durable, some nails, some tape or a stapler, and an adult to help build the birdfeeder.

Start Experimenting.

1. Are you ready to make a birdfeeder?
2. Take one of the empty cartons and wash it until it is nice and clean.
3. Now have an adult cut the carton down so you have only about an inch of the sides left all the way around. Put a small hole in each side of the carton. Loop and tie the string to the holes and hang it up. If you do not want to hang the birdfeeder, you can nail the bottom of the box to the window sill or some other place where you can still observe. You have just made one kind of birdfeeder.

4. Take the other empty carton and wash it well. Now stand the carton up and tape or staple the top shut. Have an adult cut out a small window. This should be close to the bottom of the milk carton leaving most of the top closed. Put holes in both sides of the top part of the milk carton.

Run the yarn or string through to make a hanger. You have just made another kind of birdfeeder. You can also paint or decorate your birdfeeders.
5. Put some "bird food" in the feeders.

Can you answer the following questions about birds and birdfeeders?

1. When the birds start coming to your birdfeeders how are you going to know what kind of bird you are seeing?
2. Do you think it would be a good idea to keep a notebook of the kinds of birds you are watching?
3. What do you think birds like to eat?
4. What are some important facts to consider before finding a place for your birdfeeders?
5. Do you think birds care what kind of birdfeeder you are making?
6. Do you know what your State bird is?
7. Do you know how many different kinds of birds there are? Take a guess.
8. Where would be a good place to find out more about birds so that you can name the birds you see?
9. Do you know what an Ornithologist is?

Backyard Scientist solution to experiment.

There are many things that will help you identify the kinds of birds you see. The size, shape, color and pattern of the feathers, beak, songs, calls and movements are good ways to identify birds. It is wise to keep a notebook and write down all the above characteristics so you can later identify the birds.
Birds like to eat. In fact, did you know that the smaller the bird, the more it will eat? Ornithologists are scientists who study birds, and they have found that some baby birds eat close to their own weight in food in one day alone.

It is very important to find a place for your birdfeeder where it will be easy for you to fill it each day. Make sure your birdfeeder is high enough so that cats will not be able to hurt the birds. Remember, birds are shy, so if you do place the birdfeeder on your window sill, it might take the birds a while to try it out.

In the United States, each State has its own State bird. Find out what your State bird is. There are about 9,000 different kinds of birds throughout the world of different sizes and colors. How close was your guess about how many different kinds of birds there are?

To find out what kinds of birds you are actually seeing, check an encyclopedia or bird guidebook. You can find these in the library. Birds are very interesting to study.

Remember, keep your birdfeeder supplied with seed mixtures. You can include some bread crumbs, donut crumbs, cookie crumbs, berries, nuts and also fruits. You can also find out what other foods birds like to eat. Most birds like seeds, but not all. For instance, Woodpeckers eat ants and beetles, and Puffins eat fish. It is very important to keep your birdfeeder clean. Have fun discovering birds.

THE YEAST EXPERIMENT

Can you get a bag to puff up just using yeast?

Try the following Backyard Scientist experiment to discover the answer.

Gather the following supplies:

Two 1 gallon size ziplock bags, 2 packets of dry yeast, measuring cups, 2 cookies containing sugar, 2 glass or metal baking dishes big enough to hold the ziplock bags, labels for the bags, warm water, a small bowl, and a timer or clock.

Start Experimenting.

1. Take one of the ziplock bags and label it yeast, cookies and water. Take the other ziplock bag and label this one yeast and water.
2. Put both baking dishes out so they will be ready for the experiment.
3. Take one of the ziplock bags and make sure all the air is out of it. Now take one of the packages of yeast and open it carefully over a bowl. Pour the yeast into the ziplock bag labeled yeast and water.
4. Now measure 2/3 cup warm water (test the water on your wrist, and if it feels comfortable it is the right temperature), and pour this into the bag. Seal the bag

and mix the yeast and water together by bouncing the bag up and down on the table. Take one of the baking dishes and fill it almost to the top with warm water (test water as before) from the tap. Put the ziplock bag on top of the water.

5. Take the ziplock bag labeled yeast, cookies and water. Make sure all the air is out. Open the package of yeast over the bowl and pour it into the bag. Now take the two cookies and break them in half, then in half again. Put them into the bag and add 2/3 cup warm water (test the water as before). Seal the bag and mix this up very well and squash the cookies so everything is well mixed.

6. Take the other baking pan and fill it up almost to the top with warm warm (test the water as before). Put the bag you just prepared on top of the water.
7. Now set your timer for 1/2 hour. Meanwhile, see if you can answer the following questions. It is all right to try and predict what is going to happen.

1. Which bag do you think will puff up? Why do you think this?
2. Can you name some things we use yeast for?
3. Do you think yeast is a plant?

After 1/2 hour, look at your two bags. What do you observe? Leave the bags in the water all day and keep checking on them every once in a while. You can also add a little warm water to the baking pans each time you check on the bags. Do not open the bags.

Can you answer the following questions from your observations?

1. Which bag did puff up? Did you guess correctly?
2. What did the bag that puffed up have in it that the other bag did not contain?
3. What are some of the ingredients that are in the cookies you put into the bag?
4. Where do you think the yeast got the energy it required?
5. Do you think after several hours the other bag with just the water and yeast in it will also puff up?
6. What are the little bubbles you are seeing in the bag containing the yeast, warm water and cookies?
7. Does yeast need light to grow?

Backyard Scientist solution to experiment.

Did you discover that the bag with the yeast,

cookies and warm water is getting bigger and bigger? This is because when yeast comes to life and starts growing, it gives off a gas. The gas is evidence that the yeast is living. These gas bubbles rise up in the mixture and cause, in this case, the bag to expand. If you were baking bread, the gas bubbles would cause the dough to rise. The gas it gives off is carbon dioxide, which is composed of carbon and oxygen molecules.

Yeast is made up of tiny cells. These yeast cells are single-celled organisms. Yeast does not make its own food like other plants do. In fact, yeast makes no food of its own and needs no light to survive and grow. Yeast's growth and metabolism must come from foods available to it. Yeast gets its energy from sugar. The sugar is oxidized and carbon dioxide is given off. The cookies you used had sugar in them. They contained the sugar (food source) for the yeast's growth. The reason the other bag did not puff up was because that bag contained yeast and water only. Yeast will grow best in warm temperatures. If the water is too hot, it will kill the yeast. If the water is too cold, the yeast will stop growing. You may have seen the bag with only yeast and water enlarge when it was placed in the warm water. This was only temporary and due to other scientific principles such as expansion of molecules and pressure. (See other Backyard Scientist Series of books).

Yeast is used in making bread and some alcoholic beverages.

You could try this experiment again to see if other sweets such as honey, molasses and fruit juices will provide the food sources to get yeast to grow. You can also try cookies with no sugar in them and see what happens or try an artificial sweetener. What other things can you think of to try?

THE ISOPOD EXPERIMENT

Do you know what an isopod is?

Try the following Backyard Scientist experiment to discover the answer.

Gather the following supplies:

Several friends, an adult to act as leader, several clear plastic 6 oz or 8 oz cups, several plastic bags, several sticks, several small shovels or sturdy spoons for digging, pencil and paper, chalk, several 8 1/2" x 11" pieces of paper, scotch tape, scissors, and several hand magnifying lenses.

CAUTION: There are a couple of dangerous insects that can live in the same sort of places as isopods. Watch carefully for things like scorpions, black widows or anything else you are unsure of. Always ask the adult leader when in doubt.

Start Experimenting.

You are all about to go on an isopod hunt. Isopods are small, grey or black animals with many legs. These animals have been called pill bug, potato bug, and roly-poly bug. They are found while pulling weeds or looking under rocks. A good place to find isopods is in a garden, park or a vacant lot. Isopods hang out in dark, moist undisturbed spots with decaying plant matter. This decaying matter is food for an isopod. Other good places to look for isopods are under boards, logs, rocks, piles of leaves and grass cuttings. You can even dig into the litter beneath trees to find them.

1. Gather your friends and take the plastic cups, bags, and materials for digging. Each person should try to bring back at least 4 to 8 isopods.

2. When you find an isopod, place it in your hand and put it gently into the bag or plastic cup.
3. A time limit should be set, and everyone has to be back with at least 4 isopods at that time. Go on the hunt with a partner.
4. When the time is up for collecting isopods, everyone is to meet and take out their magnifying lense, pencil and paper. Now each child is to look closely at the physical structures and the behaviors of the isopods. A structure is any part of the isopod's body (like the tail or leg), and the behavior is what an isopod does (runs, curls, turns over). List behavior and structures on the paper.
5. Do you think all isopods are alike?
6. Now it is time to race your isopods.
7. Everyone take the piece of paper, scotch tape and scissors. Roll and scotch tape the paper into a "bird beak" funnel. Cut off enough of the tip to leave a 1/2 inch opening.
8. Have someone take the piece of chalk and draw circular racetracks on the concrete or asphalt and mark the center of the racetrack. Draw one racetrack for every two children.
9. Get ready to race! Pretend your isopods are being chased by an animal that wants to capture it. Get into groups of two. Each one pick one isopod from your collection to race. Now drop the isopods through the paper "bird beak" funnel and take the funnel into the center of the racetrack. Lift up your funnel and the race is on. The first isopod to reach the outside line is the winner.
10. You can also have challenge races between winning isopods.

Can you answer the following questions from your observations?

1. Which kind of isopod won most of the races?
2. Why do you think those isopods won?
3. Do you think by racing the isopods on grass or gravel the results would be different? Try it.
4. Which isopods do you think would be easier to see in the grass? Put the isopods in the grass and discover the answer.
5. How many different kinds of isopods did you find?
6. How do you think slow isopods protect themselves?

Backyard Scientist solution to experiment.

There is more than one kind of isopod. The different isopods have different structures and behavior. A better understanding of the special characteristics and abilities of living things will develop from the above experiment. The presence, or absence, and the shape and size of structures of an organism determine the kind of things the animals can do (the wings of a bird enable it to fly). A common isopod is called the pill bug. The pill bug has a high domed body. This high domed body enables the isopod to roll into a tight protective ball when disturbed. The pill bug is generally a slower runner than other isopods and is unable to flip over from an upside-down position. Another common isopod, the sow bug, has two tail-like appendages and a broad, flattened body that allows it to flip over easily from an upside-down position onto its feet and run. The sow bug cannot roll into a ball as the pill bug does. The sow bug relies on speed to reach a place where it can hide from its predators.

When you are all finished with this investigation about isopods, return all isopods to the places where they were captured.

THE BACKBONE EXPERIMENT

Do you know how your backbone moves?

Try the following Backyard Scientist experiment to discover the answer.

Gather the following supplies:

Four regular size spools of thread (they can have thread or be empty of thread). 1 plastic straw and 1 piece of string about 12" long.

Start Experimenting.

1. Gather the four spools of thread and the plastic straw.
2. Take the 4 spools of thread and stack them on top of each other.
3. Hold the bottom spool while pressing down on top spool, and gently move it.
3. Hold the bottom spool while pressing down on top spool, and gently move it.
4. What happens?
5. Put the straw through the center of the spools.
6. Hold bottom spool and bend the top spool over to one side a little. Now straighten it. What did you notice when it was bent?

Backyard Scientist solution to above experiment.

You have just made a model of your backbone. By moving the top spool over to one side, this enabled each spool to move just a little. Now, the chain of spools can bend a lot, the same as your backbone. When you bend over, your backbone moved a lot like the model you just made.

NOTE: If there is thread on the spools, be sure the end of the thread is secured in the slot on spool. You can use the straw to push the string through the spools.

Take the four spools of thread and the piece of string, and hold the piece of string out in front of you straight up and down. Now, let go of the string. What happens? Did you find the string falls to the ground? Take the string and tie a large knot at the bottom end of the string. Thread one spool onto the string pulling knot so it sticks in spool. Thread the rest of the spools onto the string, resting the bottom spool on the table. Hold the spools straight in front of you. Then let go of the top end. What happens?

Did you find the spools and the string remain upright? The spools represent the backbone (vertebrae). The space between each vertebra on your body has an elastic type disk to allow it to bend and to absorb shock.

Did you know that some animals have backbones and some animals do not have backbones? This would be an interesting subject to research.

You could actually put a backbone together. The next time you have fish for dinner save all the bones from the backbone and clean them very well. Place them on a sheet of newspaper. Now try to put the backbone together to see how the fish moves.

THE NERVE CELL EXPERIMENT

Why are your nerve cells so important?

Try the following Backyard Scientist experiment to discover the answer.

LOCATION	DISTANCE BETWEEN TOOTHPICKS
FINGERTIP	
BACK OF HAND	
CHEEK	
BACK OF NECK	

Gather the following supplies:

One blindfold (scarf), 2 toothpicks, a ruler, a piece of white blank 8 1/2" by 11" paper, pencil, and a friend to help in the experiment. Optional, a microscope and slide.

Start Experimenting.

Before you start this experiment, make a chart, like the sample, to record your experiment.

1. Blindfold your friend. Gather the two toothpicks and, holding them together, poke your friend gently on the fingertip until your friend can feel the pressure. Ask your friend if he/she feels one or two toothpicks.

2. Now try step number one again. This time move the toothpicks slightly apart. Ask your friend how many toothpicks were felt. Keep moving the toothpicks apart until you friend feels the touch of two toothpicks.

3. Take the ruler and measure the distance between the two toothpicks and record the number on your chart.

4. Repeat the above steps on your friend's cheek, the back of the neck, and the back of the hand. When two pokes are felt, record the number on the chart.
5. Now trade places with your friend, and have your friend try all the above steps on you, recording the number each time on the chart.

Can you answer the following questions from your observations?

1. Where are the nerve cells farthest apart?
2. Why do you think they are so far apart?
3. Where are the nerve cells closest together?
4. Why do you think they are so close?
5. Do you think that testing water in the bathtub with your hands for temperature is a true test?
6. Why do you think mothers test their baby's formula on their wrists?
7. We know our skin is sensitive to touch, but can you name what else our skin does?

Backyard Scientist solution to experiment.

Did you discover that your nerve cells are the farthest apart in the back of your neck because we don't use our neck to feel many things. Did you discover that at your fingertips the nerve cells are closest together? We use our fingertips to feel many things.

When testing bath water with your hands, you will discover that the lack of nerve endings in the hands for temperature works against you. You hands will feel comfortable in the bath water and you go in. Then you discover the water is too hot for the rest of your body. You should test the bath water with your elbows, which are far more sensitive to temperature change than your hands

are. Another part of the body sensitive to temperature is the wrist. This is why mothers test the temperature of a baby's formula on their wrist. We have nerve endings to sense heat, cold, pain, pressure, light and smell to name a few. All your sense organs act together as detectives to help tell you about the world in which you live. Like your brain which helps you with reasoning and memory, the sense organs give you information about yourself and your environment.

The skin, besides sensing touch, is the fortress of the human body. The skin protects you from germs and bacteria and prevents the fluid that feeds the cells from evaporating. It also helps keep the body temperature constant.

Did you know that your skin is made up of layers very much like a package of sliced cheese? Through these layers, the blood vessels, hair and nerves grow. The top section, or "epidermis", is made up of several layers of dead cells that are stretched out and flattened. These dead cells are brushed off daily by washing and through clothing rubbing against the skin. There are no nerve endings in this layer of skin. Take your fingernail and run it over your arm, and clean out the stuff under your fingernail on a microscope slide. Now look at this through your microscope and you can see lots and lots of epidermis cells. You can use a good magnifying glass too. For further study you can read about the layer that is under the epidermis which is the "dermis" and find out what the "dermis" does.

THE LUNG EXPERIMENT

Do you know how you breathe?

Try the following Backyard Scientist experiment to discover the answer.

Gather the following supplies:

One clear 8 oz. or 10 oz. plastic cup, scissors, I large balloon, 2 small balloons, masking tape, a ball of clay, 1 straw, a ruler, rubber band, and large nail. You will also need a table top for a work area, a balloon pump (optional) and the help of an adult.

Start Experimenting.

1. Have the adult heat the nail, then with the heated nail punch a hole the size of a straw opening in the bottom of the plastic cup.
2. Measure the straw in thirds. Cut off the first third. Make a partial cut at the center of the long piece. Do not cut all the way through the straw. Cut the end of the short straw so it is pointed and looks like a screwdriver. Bend the long piece at the partial cut and insert the short straw at

the bend. Tape the straw at the junction. The edges should be airtight.
3. Slip a small balloon over each end of the Y tube and tape the edges. Push the long end of the straw through the hole in the cup. Seal the edges of the hole with clay.
4. Use the scissors to cut the bottom off of the large balloon and discard. Slip the top part over the glass after the straw is inserted into the glass. Twist the neck

tightly and put tape or a rubber band around it to hold it tightly sealed. this becomes your handle.

5. Turn the cup upside down and pull the handle down. What happens? Carefully observe what happens each time you pull the handle down and each time you let go.

Can you answer the following questions from your observations?

1. What do you think you have just made?
2. What do you think the cup represents?
3. Do you know what the Y tube stands for?
4. Now think about how you breathe.
5. Where does your breathing come from? How can your lungs be compared to the cup with the balloons in it?

Backyard Scientist solution to experiment.

You have just made a balloon model of your lungs. Inside the cup is a model of your chest or rib cage. The Y tube stands for your windpipe. Your windpipe has two branches, one to each lung, just as the Y tube has a branch going into each balloon. Did you notice that the balloons get filled with air each time you pull down on the rubber sheet? You are actually making the space in the cup bigger. When you let go of the rubber sheet, the balloons lose their air. You are actually making the space smaller by letting go of the rubber sheet when the sheet goes back up. The space in the cup gets smaller again because the air inside the cup gets pushed back into the smaller space. This air pushes against the balloons and pushes the air out of them. Your nose and throat lead incoming air to the windpipe.

The two balloons inside the cup are models of your lungs. Let's compare the way these model lungs work with the way your real lungs work. The rubber sheet is like your diaphragm. The diaphragm is a large muscle just below your rib cage. See if you can find it on yourself. This muscle moves down when you breathe in. Try it. The space in your chest gets larger. The air inside presses less. Now the greater air pressure outside pushes air into your lungs. The air comes in through your nose and mouth, or, in this case, from the straw.

Now put you hands at the bottom of your rib cage, where the diaphragm is, and take a deep breath. Do you feel your ribs sticking out? This, too, helps make the space in your chest bigger. When you breathe out, your diaphragm goes back up, as the rubber sheet did in your model. The inside of your chest gets smaller again, because air is pushed out of your lungs. So, each time you inhale you breathe in fresh air, and each time you exhale you breathe out used air. The fresh air you breathe contains oxygen. Your body changes the oxygen to carbon dioxide, a waste product which you breathe out. Your lungs help your body breathe. They are like balloons filling up with air and letting air out.

When your ribs move out, they pull your lungs with them so they open up to their fullest and suck in air. When your ribs move in, they squash the air out of your lungs. This is like pushing air out of a balloon pump. Find out how much air you breathe by pretending to be a balloon pump. How much air can you blow into a balloon with one breath?

Your lungs are in the upper part of your chest and are made up of millions of elastic like sacs which fill up and let out air. Did you know that your lungs can hold about as much air as a basketball?

THE ANT EXPERIMENT

Have you ever followed an ant?

Try the following Backyard Scientist experiment to discover the answer.

Gather the following supplies:

For this experiment, you need to go outdoors and look for ants. Ants can be found where people are having picnics, and you might see some when you are playing in your backyard or in the park. You will also need some food to attract the ants. Cookies will do fine. You will also need a magnifying glass, and some friends to go with you.

Start Experimenting.

1. Go outside with your friends and try to find some ants. If you are having trouble finding ants, put down some food and soon the ants will be coming to you.

2. When the ants start to come, watch them very carefully. Take your magnifying glass and examine one closely. Can you see three separate parts to its body? Look at the antennae, the jaws and the eyes.

3. Now look closely at the antennae.
4. Keep watching the ants and observing everything about them.
5. Follow some ants to see where they are going.
6. If the ants you are watching are following one path coming and going, rub your fingers across the earth in front of one of the ants (never touch an ant directly as it could bite). What happens to the column of ants?
7. Now see if you can find the ant nest. Sometimes the ants will lead you to a mound, or a pile of earth, with an opening in it. The nest could be under a rock or in a tree. If you think the nest is under a rock, then lift the rock and see if it is there.
8. When you find an ant's nest, what discoveries are you making about ants?

Can you answer the following questions from your observations?

1. What are the three separate parts of an ant's body?
2. To which part of the body are the legs connected?
3. Are the legs long, compared with the rest of the body?
4. Do ants move slowly or quickly?
5. What is the ant's antennae always doing?
6. Can an ant carry something larger than itself?
7. If you found a nest, what are the things you saw taking place? Were you able to tell the queen ants from the worker ants?

Backyard Scientist solution to experiment.

Did you discover that the three separate parts of an ant's body is the small head, the thin thorax, and the big abdomen? Ants have six legs, three on each side of the body. Their legs are long and an ant can run very fast for its size. The ant's antennae are always moving. An ant uses them as feelers and for smelling. Ants do not have a nose. They do have eyes but cannot see very well. Ants can carry loads that are much bigger and heavier than they are.

The kinds of ants we see most of the time are those that live in the ground. Their nest may have one or more openings. These openings are sometimes hidden by leaves or twigs. Many times these openings are easy to see. They may be found above the ground or below the ground. Often ants are crawling about near the opening of their nests.

When you rub your finger across the earth in front of one of the ants, you are putting a different chemical on the ground than the ants are used to. This could break the ant's trail, and the ants could become confused as to where to go next. Ants give off a certain chemical that is picked up on the ground. It is the way the ant is able to make a path that will enable the other ants to smell and follow this to food. It is an inborn behavior for these ants to follow this chemical, expecting food.

Now turn to the next experiment where we are going to build an ant farm.

THE ANT FARM EXPERIMENT

What do you know about building an ant farm?

Try the following Backyard Scientist experiment to discover the answer.

Gather the following supplies:

A large glass jar with a lid, some planting soil, a sifter, a thin cloth, a rubber band, a small pan of water, a piece of 8 1/2" by 11" black paper, sugar, a pair of garden gloves, a small shovel, cotton balls, a paint brush, 1 box of plaster of Paris, little pieces of apple, carrot, potato, melon, meat, vegetables, honey, sugar, bits of egg white and butter (you don't have to have all the above foods), some Vaseline and an adult to help you collect the ants.

Start Experimenting.

1. Take the jar and prepare it for the ants by first sifting the planting soil with a sifter. Now take the plaster of Paris, add a little water and make a ball about the size of a golf ball with it. Wait for the ball to harden. Put the plaster of Paris ball in the center of the jar with the sifted dirt all around it like a cylinder effect. Take the thin cloth, the rubber band, shovel, the paint brush, garden gloves and the prepared ant jar, and put all these supplies in a bag to have ready to carry with you on your ant hunt.

2. Look for lines of ants marching along sidewalks or dirt. Follow the ants to their nest.

3. Once you get to the nest, put on your garden gloves and start digging into the nest. Transfer the ant colony into the jar. You can take the paint brush and scoop up the ants, then shake them into the jar.

DON'T TOUCH THE ANTS, USE THE GARDEN GLOVES. SOME ANTS WILL BITE AND STING.

4. If you dig deep enough, you might be able to find the queen ant, who is much larger than the rest of the ants. Try and find some eggs in the ant colony to put into your jar. After you have gathered up all of the ants and eggs, cover the jar with the thin cloth and hold it in place with a rubber band.
5. Take the jar home and put it into a small pan of water.
6. Have an adult help you punch some tiny holes in the lid. Rub a little Vaseline along the rim of the lid of the jar. Now cover the jar with the lid. Take the black piece of paper and put it around the jar whenever you are not observing the ants.
7. The soil inside the jar must be kept a little moist. Every week feed the ants by sprinkling, through the holes, a few grains of sugar over the top of the soil. You can also try experimenting with different types of food listed above.
8. Soak some cotton balls in sugar water and drop them onto the dirt.
9. Watch your ants on a regular basis, and see how they live together, work together, and play together.

Can you answer the following questions from your observations?

1. Why is it important to put the jar in the water?
2. Why do you think the ants need a dark environment?
3. Why do you think we put Vaseline along the rim of the cover of the ant jar?
4. Are ants lazy or do they work hard?
5. How can you tell if the ants like a particular food that you put in the jar?
6. Do ants keep their nest clean?

Backyard Scientist solution to experiment.

It is important to put the jar in water because this will keep the ants from escaping. They will drown if they try to escape. If you left the black piece of paper off, then the ants would build their tunnels toward the center of the soil, out of sight, so you could not observe them.

If the ants like a particular food they will all gather around it.

Some kind of ants do not like any sunlight at all and only come out at night. A group of ants living together in a nest is called a colony. An ant colony has three kinds of grown-up ants: the workers, males and queens. The queen is the mother of the ants. She is also the largest, and her job is to lay eggs. Worker ants feed the queen, clean her and wait on her almost all her life. The queen could live for 15 years. The male ant does not work. He is the father of the ants. Most of the ants in a colony are worker ants. The worker ant is one of the most interesting of insects. Worker ants are easy to find and study. Ants are among the oldest insects in the world.

Ants keep their nest very clean. They will always put dead ants and other waste matter in one pile at the corner of the nest, as far away from the young ants as possible.

Now it would be fun to use your encyclopedia to draw an ant and try to identify its parts. Did you know that ants live almost everywhere in the world? They live in both cold and hot climates. Ants work and live together. They build a home, find their food, take care of the queen and her eggs, and defend their home together.

BREATHING EXPERIMENT

How much air can your lungs hold?

Try the following Backyard Scientist experiment to discover the answer.

Gather the following supplies:

One gallon glass bottle or jug (you can use a plastic container if it is transparent enough to see the water level), 2 pieces of rubber tubing about 20" long (drug stores usually have this), a marking pen, 1 piece of wax paper about 8 1/2" by 11", a sink, a large cake pan, a friend to experiment with you, and an adult to help you.

Start Experimenting.

1. Take the bottle, jug or container and thoroughly wash inside and out with soap and water.
2. Fill the bottle, jug or container with water up to the top.
3. Put the cake pan in the bottom of the sink and fill it with water.
4. Fold the wax paper several times, then have an adult hold this over the mouth of the bottle, jug or container very tightly with their hand, and turn the bottle, jug or container upside down.
5. Have the adult carefully put the upside-down jug in the pan.
6. Now slip one end of the tubing under the bottle, jug or container and into the opening. Hold the other end of the tubing in your hand.
7. Take a deep breath and exhale air through the tube and into the container. Squeeze the end of the tube shut.
8. Mark the new level of the water on the side of the bottle, jug or container.
9. Now refill the bottle, jug or container with water and let your friend have a turn. Have your friend take the other piece of rubber tubing and repeat steps 6, 7, and 8.

Can you answer the following questions from your observations?

1. How can you find out your lung capacity from this experiment?
2. When you breathe in or inhale what do you take in?
3. What are you breathing out when you exhale?
4. How does this experiment measure the air in your lungs?
5. Can you blow out all the air in your lungs?

Backyard Scientist solution to experiment.

To find out your lung capacity, empty the jug and see how many liters, or quarts of water, it takes to fill the jug to the place you marked. Our breathing system allows us to take in air and remove oxygen from it. When we exhale, we are exhaling a body waste called carbon dioxide (CO_2).

Water and air cannot be in the same space at the same time, nor can any other things. As you breath out, the air pushes the water out of the jug. The amount of water you push out is the same as the amount of air you breathe out. This is how we measure the air in our lungs. No matter how hard you blow, you cannot blow all the air out of your lungs. About 1,000 ml of air always stays in our lungs.

INVESTIGATING COMMON REFLEXES

Do you know what a common reflex is?

Try the following Backyard Scientist experiment to discover the answer.

Gather the following supplies:

A partner, a chair or bench.

Start Experimenting.

1. Ask your partner to sit on the edge of a chair or bench. Make sure the legs hang loose and the feet do not touch the floor.
2. Ask your partner to close his or her eyes. Now tap your partner just below the knee with the edge of your palm. Try tapping the elbow and some other parts of the body like the leg or arm.
3. Trade places with your partner and repeat steps one and two.
4. What just happened to you and your partner? What was the stimulus? What was the response?
5. Do you know what a response is?

Can you answer the following questions from your observations?

1. What happened when you tapped your partner's knee?
2. Do you know what a stimulus is?
3. Did you find a response at the elbow as well as the knee? What about other parts of the body?
4. Does your brain control the response that your knee gives when it is tapped?
5. Does another part of your body control the response that takes place when your knee is tapped?

Backyard Scientist solution to experiment.

When your knee and elbow was tapped, your leg and arm responded by kicking out. The brain is not involved in this knee, elbow reflex or reflex arc act. A reflex is an act that is inborn and automatic. Reflex arc are the nerve pathways, followed by a nerve impulse from stimulus, through connecting nerves in the spinal cord to response in a muscle or gland. A stimulus is a condition in the environment that causes an organism to react. The spinal cord is the place where the nerves are connected. Any nerve impulse begins at the nerve endings. These nerve endings sense the stimulus. There are nerve cells in your eyes which sense light, and there are nerve cells in your skin which sense a touch, or warmth, or cold. The tap on the knee is a stimulus, and this stimulus is sensed, or received, by a cell known as a sensory nerve cell.

The sensory nerve cell in the knee has a long nerve fiber which carries the impulses to the spinal cord. In the spinal cord, the impulse is relayed to a connecting nerve cell that receives the impulse and passes it to another nerve cell known as a motor nerve cell. The motor nerve cell's end is a muscle or gland. When the impulse reaches the leg muscle (as in the case of a tap on the knee), the leg kicks out automatically. This act is done without thinking and is part of your behavior from birth.

Did you know that your salivary glands produce saliva, an impulse that has been carried to the glands by a motor nerve? In your body, many nerve cells take part in any responsive act.

TASTE BUDS EXPERIMENT

Do you know where your taste buds are located?

Try the following Backyard Scientist experiment to discover the answer.

Gather the following supplies:

One apple cut into small cubes, 1 carrot cut into small cubes, 1 onion cut into small cubes, 1 potato cut into small cubes, celery stalk cut into small cubes, 1 pear cut in half, a blindfold, a pair of tweezers and a friend to experiment with you.

Start Experimenting.

1. Be sure to wash all the food, then have an adult cut it up according to the above directions.
2. Blindfold your friend and hold a pear under his nose, then put a piece of apple in his mouth. Ask your friend what he is eating, a pear or an apple?
3. Now change positions with your friend and repeat steps 2 and 3.

Did you discover that you thought you were eating a pear when you were really eating an apple? Your taste buds are a special group of cells mostly on the upper part of the tongue. They respond to the chemicals in food. Various parts of the tongue are sensitive to different kinds of taste. The front detects sweet and salt, and the back detects bitter tastes.

Now you are ready for the second part of this experiment.

1. Decide who will go first this time and become the taster. Blindfold the taster. The taster's nose must be closed (pinch it closed with thumb and forefinger) while tasting. One person now places, one at a time, each of the samples of apple, carrot, onion, potato, and celery on the taster's tongue. The taster should try to identify each food by only using his/her taste buds.
2. Have that person make a record of the taster's responses.
3. Change places and go through the same procedures as above, and see if the other person can identify each piece of food by taste alone. Make a record of the responses.

Can you answer the following questions from your observations?

1. Were you and your friend able to identify all the foods correctly?
2. Do you think the taste of most foods is really a combination of taste and smell?
3. When you have a cold and your nasal passages are clogged can you taste food?

Backyard Scientist solution to experiment.

Did you observe that you were able to recognize several of the foods by taste alone, but not all of them? The taste of most foods is really a combination of taste and smell. When you hold your nose while tasting, you cannot experience the characteristic smell of the food. This is why when you have a cold almost everything you eat is tasteless.

Did you know that sweet, sour, bitter and salty are the only food tastes to which the tongue is sensitive? Certain areas of the tongue react to each, because the taste buds in these areas contain nerve endings which respond strongly to a particular taste. All taste sensations other than sweet, sour, bitter and salty are caused by a combination of odor and taste.

EARTHWORMS EXPERIMENT

Are earthworms complex?

Try the following Backyard Scientist experiment to discover the answer.

Gather the following supplies:

A pad of paper, a pencil, a sheet of plastic, a ruler, several pieces of notebook paper 8 1/2" by 11" lined or unlined, 1 large jar that you can see through, a piece of black paper that will fit around the jar, soil, sand, leaves, 1 piece of plastic covering enough to cover a jar top, a flashlight, 1 plastic bowl, 1 cookie sheet, and friends to share the experiment with you.

Start Experimenting.

1. Now get ready to go on a worm hunt. Take the sheet of plastic and lay it on the ground. Dig up some soil, put it on the plastic, and search through it for earthworms.
2. When you find some earthworms, count them and make a note on the pad where you found the earthworms and how many you found. Try other places like a flower garden, rose bed, under a large stone, under wood and wherever else you think they might be found. Where did you find the most earthworms?
3. Now get some damp soil and put it on the cookie sheet. Find a large worm and put it on the cookie sheet on top of the damp soil.
4. Take the ruler and measure the earthworm as it moves along. What happens to the earthworm as it moves?
5. Take one of your pieces of paper. Take an earthworm and put it on the paper and listen carefully with your ear. What are you hearing?
6. Take the jar and put some damp soil in the jar to make a layer. On top of this put a layer of sand, and continue putting layers of soil and sand in the jar until it is nearly full.
7. Put three worms and some dead leaves on top of the soil. Now cover the jar with the sheet of plastic.
8. Make a few small holes in the plastic covering to let air in. Put the piece of black paper around the jar. Keep the worms in the dark. Wait 7 days and remove the paper. What are you

observing? Now put the earthworms back in the garden. They do not like to be kept in jars for long periods of time.

9. Take the plastic bowl and fill it with damp soil. Put four worms in the bowl and cover it with plastic. Make small holes in the plastic to let air in.
10. Wait one day and look at the bowl with the worms in it. Now lay several different kinds of leaves in the bowl and replace the plastic. Wait one day and uncover the bowl. What do you see? Now put the worms back in the garden.

Can you answer the following questions from your observations?

1. Do earthworms like damp soil or dry soil the best?
2. Do earthworms have eyes, ears or legs?
3. Do earthworms have a mouth, head and a tail?
4. Do all earthworms look alike? Are they all the same color?
5. Can an earthworm change its size? Is it always the same size?
6. When you put the earthworm on the sheet of paper, did you hear a noise? Do you know what was making this noise?
7. What did you discover about the worms that you kept in the jar for seven days?
8. When you put the worms in the bowl, how could you tell which leaves the earthworms liked best?

Backyard Scientist solution to experiment.

Did you discover that you found the most earthworms in damp soil? There are many different kinds of worms. Some are big, some are small. Earthworms are of different colors, also. The number of rings can differ.

Did you find that it was hard to get an exact measurement of the earthworm? Worms become shorter and longer as they move along.

Did you hear a scratching noise when the worm was on the piece of paper? The noise you heard is made from the bristles (hard hairs) which are on almost every segment of its body. These bristles help the worm to move along.

When you put the worms in the jar did you discover, after seven days, that the worms made burrows and they mixed up the layers of sand and soil? The leaves that you put on the top had been dragged down by the worms into their burrows.

When you put the worms in the bowl, did you notice the leaves they liked best were pulled down into their burrows so they could eat them?

The best time to find earthworms is in the summer when the soil is damp and warm. When it is very cold, earthworms will not go near the top of the soil. They bury themselves deep into the ground for more warmth. During the day earthworms stay in their burrows. They come out at night. If you shine a flashlight on the worms, they will go down to their burrows. Earthworms have no eyes. They can feel the light shining on them because of special cells in their skin. Earthworms do not have ears or legs. They do have a mouth, a head and a tail.

Did you know that earthworms need to stay moist? It is important to have earthworms in gardens because the holes they make are good for plants. They also add nutrients to the soil by digesting food and depositing the refuse from the digestive process. Air and water can enter the soil easily and help the plants to grow better. There are many other interesting things to find out about earthworms. You might want to do some more research.

THE SOIL EXPERIMENT

Is all soil the same?

Try the following Backyard Scientist experiment to discover the answer.

Gather the following supplies:

One paper cup, some soil, access to water, a long spoon or stirring sticks, 1 magnifying glass, labels, a marking pen, several empty jars (baby food jars work well for this) and a friend to experiment with you.

1. Go out to your yard and pick up a handful of soil. Now look at it very carefully. What do you think soil is made of?
2. Rub a small amount of the soil between your fingers. How does it feel? What does the texture of the soil look like?
3. Take your jars and go on a soil hunt. Collect samples of soil from the beach, park, your yard, a friend's yard, a vacant lot, fields, woods, swamps and any other place where you can collect soil. Label the soil containers as you collect. After you have collected all your soil samples, place at least two inches of soil in each jar and label the jars telling where the soil was collected.
4. Add water to the jars of soil until each jar is 3/4 full. Now stir the soil and water together. Let the soil settle down in the water for at least 1/2 hour. What are you observing? Do you see things floating on the top of the water?

Can you answer the following questions from your observations?

1. What do you think soil is made of?
2. Do soils all have the same textures?
3. Are all the soils you collected the same?
4. When you added water to the soil and it settled down, what were you observing?
5. What was floating on top of the water in your jars?
6. Why is it important for scientists to know about the different kinds of soil?
7. If you had sandy soil, clay soil and loam soil (humus soil), which soil would you use for your planting?

Did you notice when you picked up some soil from your yard, you saw a mixture of very small pieces of rock and rooted materials from plants and animals; such as dead leaves, twigs, stems and parts of insects and other animals? This kind of soil is called loam soil (humus soil).

Soils have different textures depending on the size of rocks in them and the other materials in them. Some soils feel gritty, some feel smoother. In sandy soils, you can see rock particles with your eyes. In silty soils, you can see the particles with a hand lens. In clay soils, the particles are even too small to see with a magnifying glass.

Did you notice that when you put the different soils you collected into the jars with the water, you could see some of the smallest particles being held up by the water for a long time? These tiny particles are clay and turn the water cloudy. The cloudier the water, the more clay particles are in the soils. The bits of plant and animal materials that are floating on top of the water are parts of the humus in the soil. Humus is formed when decayed plants and animals become part of the soil. The gravel and sand in the soil settle on the bottom.

Now compare the various soils from the different sites. Do you see more humus particles in the park soil or in the sand? Which one of the soils have more clay in it? What other differences can you notice in the soils? You might want to make a chart and note the differences you are observing.

THE SOIL TEST

Do you know what kind of crops will grow better in one soil than another?

Try the following Backyard Scientist experiment to discover the answer.

Gather the following supplies:

Three jars, all the same size, that you can see through, clay soil, garden soil (humus soil), sand, a pitcher to pour water from, a tin can (soup size or larger) with both ends removed from the can and edges smoothed, and a watch.

Start Experimenting.

1. Put labels on each jar for the clay soil, garden soil and sand.
2. Now take the clay soil and pack it into the jar labeled clay soil.
3. Take the garden soil (humus) and pack it into the jar labeled garden soil.
4. Now take the sand and pack it into the jar labeled sand.
5. Pour 1/4 cup of water on top of each sample.
6. Observe what is happening to each sample.

Can you answer the following questions from your observations?

1. What differences did you notice when you poured the water into each sample you were testing?
2. From this test which sample would you use for topsoil when you plant something?
3. If topsoil is destroyed, can it be rebuilt easily?
4. Why do you think this test is important?

Backyard Scientist solution to experiment.

Did you discover that the sandy soil lets water pass through too quickly, and clay soil holds water but tends to cake? The humus (garden) soil holds just enough water for plants to grow in, while letting the water spread throughout the soil.

Did you know that once a good topsoil is destroyed, it takes a long time to rebuild it, if at all?

It is very important for soil scientists to conduct tests on different kinds of soils. The information gathered from these tests will help farmers know what kind of crop will grow better in one soil than another. Knowing about soils will help farmers to prevent soil erosion and protect their soil for crops. Scientists, through their studies, can try to improve the soil so that a particular crop can be planted in it. In other cases, scientists try to improve the plants, so the plants can live in the poorer soil.

Now take the tin can and make sure both ends are removed and the edges smoothed. Wash it very well. Take the empty tin can out to your yard (first get permission), and push the bottom of the can down one inch into the soil. Fill the can with water. Take the watch and see how long it takes for the water to go into the soil. Try this same method in different places around your house. A bare spot in a path, a lot, under a tree, near a flower bed, or at a friend's house (always getting permission to do this). Take notes or write down how long it takes for the water to soak into the soil at each spot. Also observe which soil appears to dry the fastest.

THE EAR EXPERIMENT

Do you really need both ears to hear?

Try the following Backyard Scientist experiment to discover the answer.

Gather the following supplies:

Some sterile cotton (the kind that comes in a box from the drug store), a loud ticking clock or a timer that makes a loud noise, or a portable radio, 1 small bottle (soft drink bottles are good for this), 1 glass, 1 funnel, some water, and a friend to share the experiment with you.

Start Experimenting.

1. Put some cotton into the outer part of one of your ears. Have your friend, without you seeing her/him, hide the clock or timer or the radio (with music playing) somewhere in the room.

2. Now close your eyes and see if you can find where the noise or music is coming from with just your hearing alone.

3. Take the cotton out of your ear, and see if you still have trouble finding where the sounds are coming from.

4. Trade places with your friend and hide the clock, timer or radio, and have your friend do steps 1, 2 and 3.
5. Take the bottle and the glass over to the sink and fill the glass with water. This experiment has to be done over the sink.
6. Try to pour water from the glass into the bottle.
7. Now take the funnel and put it over the bottle.
8. Fill the glass with water again.
9. Pour the water from the glass into the funnel and into the bottle.

Can you answer the following questions from your observations?

1. Were you able to tell where the ticking or music sound was coming from while the cotton was in your ear?
2. Were you able to tell where the ticking or music sound was coming from without the cotton in your ear?
3. Why is pouring water into the bottle using the funnel similar to what happens when sound waves reach our ears?
4. Does your brain play a part in your hearing?
5. Now swallow, chew or yawn. What are you feeling?
6. Have you ever had a popping sensation when you were in an airplane or driving in the mountains? Why do you think this happened?

Backyard Scientist solution to experiment.

Did you discover that having two ears is better than having one? Having two ears helps you tell what direction sounds are coming from. This is because the sound hits one ear a fraction of a second before the other and produces stronger vibrations. This gives your brain a clue to direction. The sound closest to the ear is loudest. Your

head gets in the way of sound waves approaching the other ear.

The part of the ear we see acts like a funnel to collect sound waves. It then brings them into the narrow inside canal of the ear. The wide part of the funnel in the above experiment collected the water and then directed it right into the narrow neck of the bottle.

Look closely at the word hear. Do you see the word "ear" in it? Your ears can hear very loud sounds and very soft sounds.

The part of your ear that you can see catches all kinds of sounds. It sends the sounds to the rest of your ear, which is inside your head. Your ears change the sounds into messages that nerves can understand. These nerve messages are then sent to your brain. Your brain tells you what you heard.

The only way that air can get into or out of your middle ear is through the Eustachian tube. When you swallow, chew or yawn, the entrance to the tube opens and air can pass in or out. This allows the air pressure on both sides of your ear drum to remain equal. The pressure outside your ear sometimes changes suddenly when you are in an airplane. For example, the popping sensation you get is the pressure equalizing in your middle ear. Swallowing helps to equalize it more quickly.

It would be fun to draw a picture of an ear. Look in the encyclopedia and label all the parts.

THE LEAF EXPERIMENT

Why are leaves important to plants?

Try the following Backyard Scientist experiment to discover the answer.

Gather the following supplies:

One healthy potted plant with green leaves (a geranium plant is good), 1 piece of aluminum foil about 6" X 6", 2 Tbsp. of Vaseline, 1 ink pad, 6 sheets of plain white paper 8 1/2" by 11", 6 different kinds of leaves, and 1 magnifying glass.

Start Experimenting.

1. Take the potted plant and set it where it will get a great deal of sunlight.
2. Cover one of the leaves of the plant completely with the piece of aluminum foil.
3. Now cover another leaf of the plant completely with Vaseline on both sides. Leave the Vaseline and aluminum foil on the leaves for ten days.
4. In ten days remove the foil. What has happened to the leaf? Has it changed in any way?
5. What happened to the leaf with the Vaseline on it after ten days?
6. Now you are ready to make a leaf print. Go outside and gather up six different kinds of leaves.
7. Take the ink pad and one of the leaves you collected, and put the leaf face down onto the ink pad. Take one of the pieces of paper and rub the paper over the leaf. Now put a clean piece of paper down and remove the paper and leaf from the ink pad putting the leaf on the piece of clean paper. Lightly press the leaf, and a clear print of the leaf will appear.
8. Repeat the step above with all the leaves you have collected. When you have made all your leaf prints, study them with a magnifying glass.

Can you answer the following questions from your observations?

1. What do you think will happen to the leaf covered with the aluminum foil?
2. What do you think will happen to the leaf covered with Vaseline?
3. Why is a leaf important to a plant?
4. Is it important for a leaf to get air?
5. Is it important for a leaf to have light?

6. When you examined the leaf prints with the magnifying glass, what did you observe in the leaves?

Backyard Scientist solution to experiment.

After ten days when you removed the aluminum foil from the leaf, you discovered the leaf was a yellowish brown and did not look very healthy. It is important for the leaves to stay healthy and green because the leaves of a plant make food for the plant. A plant cannot live without its leaves. This process of food making is called photosynthesis. The carbohydrates produced are used and stored by the plant and, in the process, oxygen is released into the air. This process occurs only in plants containing chlorophyll. The energy from sunlight is needed to make chlorophyll. Chlorophyll is the chemical that gives plants their green color.

Now examine the leaf with the Vaseline on it. This leaf also turned a yellowish brown. The Vaseline kept the air from reaching the leaf. A plant needs carbon dioxide from the air. The carbon dioxide enters the leaves through tiny openings in them. When a leaf does not get carbon dioxide, it cannot make food, and without food the leaf will die.

After examining your leaf prints, you will discover that each leaf has a thin covering, or skin, on both sides to protect it. This skin is made of tiny cells. There are openings in the skin where the plant's leaf gets air. You will also see veins in the leaves. The veins in leaves form different patterns in the various kinds of leaves. The veins carry water and minerals to the leaves. Leaves are different shapes. Some are big, some small, some rounded and some pointed. After collecting a lot of leaves, you might want to get a book from the library and identify the different leaves you collected by name.

THE POPCORN EXPERIMENT

Can you grow a popcorn plant using a paper towel and plastic cup?

Try the following Backyard Scientist experiment to discover the answer.

Gather the following supplies:

One 8 oz. or 10 oz. plastic drinking glass, an eyedropper, a few sheets of paper towels, 14 kernels of popcorn, water, 4 oz. paper cup, 1 hand magnifying lens, pencil and paper.

SPECIAL NOTE: START THIS EXPERIMENT THE NIGHT BEFORE

Start Experimenting.

1. The night you start this experiment, take the small cup and fill it with water. Now put all 14 kernels of popcorn into the cup. Let the kernels soak in the cup overnight.
2. The next day take four of the kernels from the cup and carefully split them in half

and, using your magnifying glass, look very closely at them. You will see the embryo in the center part of the grain that grows into a new plant. At the top of the embryo, there is an embryo bud which is called the "plumule". This grows into the stem and leaves. Opposite the plumule is the embryo root which will form the root system. Around the plumule and embryo root is the seed leaf, which is called the "cotyledon". Around the cotyledon is the part called "endosperm". You will learn how all these functions perform as the kernels start growing.

3. Wet some paper towels and stuff them loosely in the glass.
4. Now take the seeds out of the cup they were soaking in, and carefully place the soaked seeds between the paper and the walls of the glass.
5. Watch very carefully everyday and note the changes that are taking place. This process could take up to two weeks or more. Be sure you keep the paper towels moist by adding drops of water. The plants need it.

Can you answer the following questions from your observations?

1. In three to five days after planting, what do you see emerging?
2. After six days, do you see the plumule growing into a sprout?
3. Keep watching your plant every day for changes taking place. Are you observing more roots forming? What do you see coming out of the roots? Be sure to use your magnifying glass to closely examine all the changes each time.
4. When do you know that you have a tiny popcorn plant emerging?
5. Do you think you can keep the popcorn plant in the glass indefinitely?
6. From watching this popcorn plant for several days, do you now know what the function of the embryo is?
7. What does the embryo bud grow into?
8. What does the cotyledon and the endosperm contain that is needed for the growth of the popcorn plant?

9. Do you know why this plant is actually growing?

Backyard Scientist solution to experiment.

The embryo is in the center of the kernel. This grows into a new plant. The embryo bud grows into stems and leaves and is called the "plumule." Opposite it is the embryo root that will form the root system. Around the plumule and embryo root is the seed leaf, which is called the "cotyledon." Around the cotyledon is the part called the "endosperm". Both the cotyledon and the endosperm have a lot of starch and some protein. When you plant the seed and the water enters, the food is used by the embryo as it grows. In three to five days, you will see a small root emerging. In another day, you should see the plumule growing out into a sprout that will become the stems and leaves. Now more roots form. If you look very closely, you can see tiny little root hairs coming out of the roots. They are especially clear near the sprout. Water can enter easily and travel through the root hairs into the root. There it enters special canals that carry the water to the rest of the plant. The first leaves form, and more roots appear below. You now have a tiny popcorn plant.

There is a limit to how big the popcorn plant can get in a drinking glass. If you want to find out more about the growth of the popcorn plant, you must plant it in soil. You can plant this in a vegetable garden or in a ten-inch clay pot. For planting the popcorn plant you can use ordinary potting soil. Lighten the soil by adding sand or peat moss. A mixture of half potting soil, and half sand or peat moss makes a good light soil for growing the popcorn plant.

THE PULSE EXPERIMENT

Do you think you can actually see your pulse rate?

Try the following Backyard Scientist experiment to discover the answer.

Gather the following supplies:

Your hand, a small ball of clay, chewing gum or silly putty and a toothpick.

Start Experimenting.

1. Feel your pulse by placing the first two fingers of your right hand on the side of your left wrist just below your thumb. Do not use the thumb to feel your pulse because the thumb's own pulse beat will interfere. Sometimes the pulse is hard to find, so you will have to search around for it a few times. If you don't feel anything, then do 20 jumping jacks and try again to find your pulse.
2. Take the ball of clay, gum or silly putty and put this directly over the spot where your pulse feels the strongest.
3. Stick the toothpick into the clay, gum or silly putty,(halfway so it doesn't stick you) and watching your pulse, observe what is happening to the toothpick. Remove the toothpick from the clay, gum or silly putty.
4. Now jog in place for one minute and replace the toothpick in the clay, gum or silly putty on your wrist, and watch what is happening to the toothpick in the clay on your wrist when you are done exercising.

Can you answer the questions from your observations?

1. Did you find your pulse rate? Was your pulse rate easier to detect after you did the jumping jacks?
2. When you jogged in place for one minute and replaced the toothpick, what happened to the toothpick?
3. What is the beat you feel when you take your pulse?
4. What other places on your body can you also feel your pulse?
5. Does your pulse rate go faster when you are exercising? If so, why?
6. Are children's pulse rates higher or lower than adults?

Backyard Scientist solution to experiment.

You should have been able to find your pulse rate, especially after exercising. The clay, gum or silly putty with the toothpick in it swayed back and forth, and it even swayed faster when your pulse rate increased with activity. Your pulse rate goes up when you are exercising. When you exercise, cells use more energy and so need to be supplied with more food and oxygen. These are provided to your cells by your blood as it circulates through your body. Your blood rushes through your arteries in stops and starts. The surge of blood at each beat is felt as a pulse. This surge can be felt at the neck, temple, ankle and wrist. The beat you feel in your wrist is due to the contraction of your heart, which is a muscle.

Children often have a higher pulse rate then adults because the cells of growing youngsters require more food and oxygen.

Now it would be fun to see what your pulse rate is. To do this, ask a friend to help. First find the correct position for feeling your pulse. Ask your friend to signal the beginning and end of one minute. During this minute, count the number of times your pulse beats. This will give you your pulse rate.

THE VEGETABLE AND FRUIT EXPERIMENT

Do you think there is a large quantity of water in vegetables and fruits?

Try the following Backyard Scientist experiment to discover the answer.

OUTLINE

Gather the following supplies:

One large lettuce leaf, a spinach leaf, a plate, a large slice of potato, apple, orange, and cucumber, several pieces of plain white paper 8 1/2" by 11", and a pencil.

Start Experimenting.

1. Take the large lettuce leaf and put it on a plate. Leave the plate where it won't be disturbed for 24 hours.
2. Watch the lettuce leaf very closely noting any changes you see during the day.
3. Have an adult cut a slice of potato, apple, orange and cucumber. Have a spinach leaf ready.
4. Now place each fruit and vegetable slice and the spinach leaf on a separate piece of white paper.
5. Take the pencil and trace their shapes on each piece of paper.
6. Carefully move these to a place where they won't be disturbed for three days. Make sure the slices stay inside the outlines you drew.

Can you answer the following questions from your observations?

1. After one day did the lettuce leaf get smaller or larger?
2. Does the lettuce leaf look fresh or wilted?
3. After three days, are the fruits and vegetables the same size as their outlines?
4. Do you think they weigh less or more now?
5. Where did the water go that was inside these slices of fruits and vegetables?
6. How do you think the water gets into fruits and vegetables?
7. If you have a small scale, weigh all the fresh food items, and then weigh them again at the end of the observation period. Do they weigh the same, more or less?

Backyard Scientist solution to experiment.

Did you discover the lettuce leaf wilted and grew smaller as the water in the leaf evaporated?

Did you discover that the slices of fruits and vegetables have dried and are smaller then the outlines you drew? They actually shrank and some of their shapes may have also changed.

The water inside these fruits and vegetables evaporated into the air. This loss made them smaller and they lost some of their weight. Did you know that lettuce contains as much as 95% water? Water is very necessary to sustain life.

The water that plants absorb help them to grow. When animals eat plants, the animals get the water in the plants. When you eat foods from animals like eggs, milk and meat, you are also actually eating the water in them. The water in plants and animal foods comes from drops of water that once fell from the clouds. You not only eat water, but you also drink it. We all need water to stay alive and healthy. Over half your weight is water.

THE ROOT EXPERIMENT

Do all roots grow down? Do some roots grow up?

Try the following Backyard Scientist experiment to discover the answer.

Gather the following supplies:

Six bean seeds, any size cardboard box with dividers and lid (ask a grocery store manager for this, if you don't have one), 1 small planting pot, a bag of potting soil, a roll of masking or regular tape, and an adult to help you.

Start Experimenting.

1. Put some potting soil into the small pot, and plant the seeds in the soil. Now water it well.
2. Take the cardboard box and have an adult cut holes about 2 inches across in the dividers of the box to make a maze. Now make one hole in the outside wall of the box.
3. Place the pot of seeds in the box at the side opposite the hole in the outside wall.
4. Close the lid and tape it so that no light can get through the lid.
5. Now place the box with the outside hole facing a sunny window.
6. Every few days you will have to open the box to water the seeds. After watering the seeds, be sure you re-tape the box each time.
7. After your plants grow for about 10 days, answer the following questions.

Can you answer the following questions from your observations?

1. Do you think the growing stems will find their way through the maze to the outside of the box?
2. What does this experiment tell you about the stems responding to light?
3. Are plants sensitive to gravity?
4. Which way do roots always grow?
5. Which way do stems always grow?
6. If you were to plant a seed upside down what do you think would happen to the seed?
7. Can you name three things that are important for a plant's survival?
8. How does food get into the leaves of plants?

Backyard Scientist solution to experiment.

The growing stems will find their way through the maze to the outside of the box. The stems respond to the light by growing towards it. Roots always grow down and stems always grow up, because they are both sensitive to the force of gravity. These are the behaviors of most green plants. Behaviors are what a living thing does in adapting to its environment. These behaviors are inborn and part of a plant from the very beginning of its life.

If you were to plant a seed upside down, the roots would begin growing from the top of the seed and the stem would come out from the bottom. They would both turn around because a root always grows towards gravity and a stem grows away from it. So, no matter which way you plant a seed, it will grow in the right direction. The next time you plant a shoot, try turning it on its side, or leave it in the dark for a few days keeping it well watered. What do you think will happen to the shoot?

Plants need gravity, light and water for their survival. Did you know that plants grow towards favorable conditions and away from unfavorable conditions?

Plants use the energy of light to produce food in their leaves which enables them to grow.

Try this experiment again and place some small rocks below the root end of the seed. Will the rocks block the root and keep it from growing?

THE CALCIUM EXPERIMENT

What happens when you remove minerals from bones?

Try the following Backyard Scientist experiment to discover the answer.

Gather the following supplies:

Two cooked chicken drumstick bones that have been cleaned of all the meat, 2 jars, 2 labels, tape, vinegar, water and paper towels.

NOTE: THIS EXPERIMENT CAN TAKE UP TO TWO WEEKS TO COMPLETE.

Start Experimenting.

1. Fill one jar 3/4 full with water and label it "water". Fill the second jar 3/4 full with vinegar and label it "vinegar".
2. Place one clean chicken bone in each jar. Before placing the bones in the jars, observe if the bones feel hard or soft.
3. Place the jars in a place where they will not be disturbed for a week.
4. After a week, remove the chicken bone from the jar of water. After washing and drying it, try to bend the bone. Does it bend? Leave this bone next to the water jar. Now remove the chicken bone from the jar of vinegar. After washing and drying it, try to bend the bone. Does it bend? If the bone that was in the vinegar solution doesn't bend easily, then the bone was not in the solution long enough. Repeat the process and put the bones back into their two jars for another week adding fresh water and vinegar.

Can you answer the following questions from your observations?

1. Which chicken bone was softer, the one placed in water, or the one placed in vinegar?
2. Do you know what makes bones hard and firm?
3. What effect did the vinegar have on the bone?
4. Where do we get the minerals that our bodies need?

Backyard Scientist solution to experiment.

You will discover the chicken bone that was in the vinegar solution became rubbery and was easily bent. The other chicken bone that was in the water solution remained stiff. Both bones were hard and stiff when you put them into the two solutions. Bones are hard and firm due chiefly to the calcium phosphate they contain which is not soluble in water, but is slowly changed by the acetic acid of vinegar into soluble calcium acetate. The vinegar dissolved the minerals that make bones hard. As the bone loses its calcium phosphate, it loses its stiffness and becomes flexible. You should eat foods that contain minerals to build strong bones. We get many of the minerals we need from fruits and vegetables.

Vinegar taken into the stomach is not harmful to your bones, because when ingested, it can never reach the bones as an acid. Your digestive system changes foods you ingest into things it can use to keep you strong and healthy.

EXTRAS...

Get your official Backyard Scientist Certificate and join the Backyard Scientist Club! Just print
your name on a slip of paper and state you have completed all the experiments in the book. Be
sure to enclose postage for first class mail and we will send you your official Backyard Scientist
Certificate and enroll you in the Backyard Scientist Club. Also, The Backyard Scientist would
like to know which experiments you liked best and why. Write to: **Backyard Scientist, P.O.
Box 16966, Irvine, CA 92713.**

GET READY FOR MORE ADVENTURES WITH HANDS-ON SCIENCE EXPERIMENTS IN:

"The Original Backyard Scientist"
Experiments for
Ages 4 through 12 years

"Backyard Scientist, Series One"
Experiments for
Ages 4 through 12 years

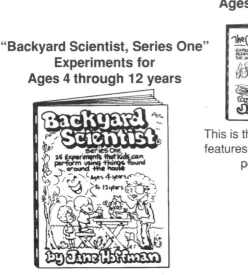

This is the author's first book and it
features many of the author's most
popular experiments.

"Backyard Scientist, Series Two
Experiments for
Ages 9 through 14 years

This is the author's second book of
fascinating and fun ways to explore the
world of science. This book is the
beginning of a series of science books.

This is the author's third book featurin
a special collection of exciting, fascinating and challenging experiments fo
children 9 through 14 years.

How to Order **"THE ORIGINAL BACKYARD SCIENTIST", "BACKYARD SCIENTIST, SERIES
ONE" and "BACKYARD SCIENTIST, SERIES TWO".**
Send check or money order for $9.50 for each book ordered, this includes shipping. California
residents add .59¢ sales tax. Send to:

BACKYARD SCIENTIST
P.O. Box 16966
Irvine, CA 92713